Café Society

A Play

Ayshe Raif

Samuel French – London
New York – Sydney – Toronto – Hollywood

CAFÉ SOCIETY

First performed at the Soho Poly, London, in November 1981 with the following cast of characters:

Amy	Barbara Ewing
Dolly	Maggie Ford
Hetty	Ann Windsor

The play directed by Cordelia Monsey

CHARACTERS

Dolly, aged 77
Hetty, aged 74
Amy, aged 72
Waitress (non-speaking part)

All the characters are Cockney, although not excessively so

The action takes place in a café in Hackney

Time: the present

CAFÉ SOCIETY

SCENE 1

The interior of a café in Hackney. Tuesday morning

The only essential pieces of furniture are a table and three chairs, and a serving counter. Further dressing can be added at the producer's discretion to suggest the café's interior

A waitress (non-speaking part) is behind the counter. Dolly, a Cockney lady of seventy-seven, is sitting alone. She has been reading her copy of the "Hackney Gazette", but her mind is not on it. She puts the paper down, sighs and stirs her tea

Hetty, a similar Cockney lady aged seventy-four, enters, puffing

Hetty Hello, dear. Oh, me legs. (*She sits heavily*) Ah, that's better. It's them stairs. Doing me legs in they are.

Dolly (*seriously*) Do you know, they're going to close this caff down, next week.

Hetty Eh?

Dolly We'll have to find somewhere else, Het. Can't meet in here no more. They've sold up.

Hetty Ah yes, there's no comfort for us old 'uns, dear. Do you think anyone cares? No. Us old 'uns are no use.

Dolly They're going to make it a "booqie".

Hetty Eh?

Dolly A dress shop.

Hetty Tut, tut. And where am I supposed to go for me breakfast? They don't care do they, dear? (*To the counter*) Tea please, lady.

Dolly Do you know, there's a nice little caff in Mare Street. Been there once.

Hetty Oh, that's a long way, Dolly, to Mare Street.

Dolly 'Course it's not. There's a lovely woman there what runs it. Italian I think she is.

Hetty I couldn't get to Mare Street, dear. Not with my legs.

Dolly Well do you know, you couldn't get there without them.

Dolly and Hetty chuckle at this bad joke. The waitress approaches with the cup of tea and plonks it down on the table

Hetty (*looking after the waitress*) Here, is it true they're going then?

Dolly I just said didn't I. They're packing up.

Hetty What do they want to go and do that for?

Dolly Can't make a living she says. Rates going up, no trade, she says.

Hetty Oh dear. (*She pauses to think*) But I always have me breakfast in here don't I, Dolly?

Dolly (*ignoring her and looking to the door*) Where is she now do you think?

Hetty Me stomach's been playing me up again.

Dolly She knows we're here by eleven.

Hetty I was up half the night again. Don't sleep so good anyhow.

Dolly Well, if you won't take your medicines, Het!

Hetty Bah! They're no good, none of 'em. (*Sighing*) I'm not long for this world, dear, that's what it is.

Dolly (*angrily*) Don't talk so daft! (*She pauses*) Perhaps she isn't coming.

Hetty Who, dear?

Dolly Amy.

Hetty Oh. Do you think I should eat something? Maybe I should. (*To the counter*) Here lady, I'll have a fried sausage and a slice of bread. (*To Dolly*) I think I could eat a bit.

Dolly (*sighing*) Do you know, those kids were putting lighted matches through my letterbox last night. I've told the Welfare, afore I come in here, not that they'll do much.

Hetty Tut, tut. The kids are terrible round here. Got no respect for us, little devils.

Dolly It's their parents I blame. Teach 'em nothing. Don't care what they get up to so long as they keep out their way.

Hetty (*not listening to Dolly*) Yes, terrible round here. I want to move away, but do you think they'll help? I keep writing to 'em but they don't take no notice of us old 'uns.

Dolly Don't keep on, Het. You don't want to go moving away at your age!

Hetty But it's no good for me. I'm not settled and I can't have a pet. It's hard living on your own with nothing for company. You're all right, you've got your Fluffy.

Dolly She's good company. Do you know, it costs me over two pound a week to feed her, but it's worth it.

Hetty You see. I've got no-one.

Dolly You've got your sister.

Hetty Daisy? She won't have me. Says they'll cut our pensions if we live together.

Dolly It's because or her I don't go away you know.

Hetty Who, dear?

Dolly My cat. Fluffy.

Hetty (*accusingly*) You're always going off on outings with your club.

Dolly For the day I do. I leave her food and water out and she's all right. I wouldn't go for a week though.

Hetty I don't even get out for the day.

Dolly You should join a club.

Hetty No, dear, I don't like them clubs.

Dolly Have you been to any?

Hetty No, but . . .

Dolly Well then!

Hetty All the same. I don't want to go to no clubs.

Dolly Don't complain then.

The waitress plonks down a plate on the table containing Hetty's sausage and bread. Hetty eats with her fingers

    Amy enters. She is wearing make-up and bright youthful clothes, despite her age of seventy-two

Amy Cooee!

Dolly You're here then.

Amy Well I'm not there am I?

Hetty Where, dear?

Amy (*amused but exasperated*) Oh, Het!

Dolly Do you know, I thought what if she's ill, and all on her own.

Amy (*sitting down*) Why should I be ill? I'm in the best of health. (*To the counter*) Tea please, ducks.

Dolly (*doggedly*) Well, we'd miss you if you fell ill.

Amy (*annoyed*) Oh, don't talk nonsense. I'm as fit now as when I was forty. It's all that dance practice we used to do. I'd be fit to drop sometimes but we'd carry on. We really learnt our craft in them days. Not like now; any old rubbish can get on the stage now.

The waitress brings Amy's tea

Dolly (*persistently*) Do you know, you can get a telephone put in by Social Services.

Amy Look, if I want a phone, ducks, I can put it in meself! I'm not so far gone I have to rely on them people.

Hetty What people, dear?

Amy Social Services.

Hetty Are they the ones who do meals on wheels? It don't agree with me, the food they bring. Most times I don't even touch it. Not at all. It's me stomach you see.

Dolly (*to Amy*) It's not charity you know. Only what you're entitled to.

Amy Well, there's no sense in taking what I don't need is there? Anyway, you've got to remember I'm not so old as you.

Dolly Huh! Five years difference.

Amy (*affronted*) I'm sixty-five!

Dolly You're seventy-two.

Amy That's a lie! I ask you, do I look seventy-two?

Dolly That's not the point is it? (*She pauses*) You started off when you was sixteen didn't you?

Amy That's right. *Dick Whittington*, Margate Empire. I was the best cat they'd ever had and they all says how good I was and how I proved meself so young!

Dolly Well, do you know that picture you showed me last week, that one of you in that outfit?

Amy nods suspiciously

It was stamped nineteen twenty-seven on the back. So you can go fibbing to your men friends, but don't you lie to me, Amy Johnson, 'cause I ain't having any!

There is a pause while Amy sulks, Dolly drinks her tea and Hetty comes out of her thoughts

Hetty I think I should have a bit more. (*To the counter*) Could I have a fried egg, lady, and a slice? (*Turning to the others*) There's not much on the telly these days is there, dear? (*She pauses*) Did you see that what was on the other night? Elsie set her settee afire.

Oh dear, you should have seen the smoke. Hilda got her out, just
in time I reckon 'cause they say that smoke can kill you. (*She
ponders*) Just think of that, dear, if Hilda hadn't got her out. I
feel sorry for that poor Hilda. She's always working hard and
that husband of hers don't help. Lazy sod he is, but it's a shame
isn't it, dear?

Amy Oh, do shut up, Hetty. It's not real you know.

Hetty What do you mean?

Dolly Never mind.

The waitress brings Hetty's food and Hetty turns her attention to it

(*To Amy*) Do you know, Amy, they're going to shut this caff
down.

Amy Oh, why?

Dolly No trade she says. They're off next week. What shall we do?

Amy What do you mean?

Dolly Where shall we meet?

Amy Oh. (*Evasively*) What's happening to this place then?

Hetty It's to be a dress shop.

Amy Typical isn't it? All the old places closing down, all the
characters moving away. There's no atmosphere no more. No
friendly hellos, no cheerful faces.

Hetty No-one wants us old 'uns, dear.

Amy It used to be great down here. They all knew me. Used to
come to see me when I was on at the Astoria, whistling and
shouting "Good on you, Amy" and "Where's our girl". Life was
good then. Why you couldn't walk ten paces without seeing a
friendly face. (*She sighs*) It used to take me half an hour to get
from one end of Chatsworth Road to the other.

Dolly (*dryly*) It takes me that now. Look, there's a lovely little caff
in Mare Street. It's not so far and the woman there's ever so nice.
I-talian I think she is.

Amy Hmm. Guess who I've seen this morning?

Dolly One of your men friends I suppose.

Amy Harry Kingham.

Hetty Who's that, dear?

Dolly Harold Kingham. Dora's Harold, you remember.

Hetty Oh, yes. Poor Dora. Dropped down dead in Clarence Road
two years ago. They said it was her heart but I reckon it was them
flats. They'll be the death of me too, see if they ain't. I wrote to

Daisy to have me 'cause she's got that big house to herself. Sisters should stick together I says. Only I don't suppose she'll have me on account of her pension, so I wrote to the Housing.

Amy Don't go on so much, Het. I want to tell you about my Harry.

Dolly *Your* Harry?

Amy Yes. He's quite sweet on me. Shouldn't be surprised if . . .

Dolly Harold Kingham soured long time since. He went daft when he lost his Dora. Anyway, you should know better at your age.

Amy What do you mean at my age? Just 'cause you're past it don't mean everyone is.

Dolly Don't be revolting!

Hetty Past what, dear?

Dolly ⎫
            } (*together*) Never mind!
Amy ⎭

Dolly At any rate, you don't want to go wasting your time with Harold Kingham.

Amy I never waste my time.

Hetty Do you think they'll move me? My neighbours are terrible. Never a good morning or how are you. Kids banging on the walls all night. I'll have to move.

Dolly I think we should try that caff in Mare Street.

The Lights fade to a Black-out

SCENE 2

The same. Wednesday

Dolly and Hetty are sitting at their table drinking cups of tea

Dolly (*firmly*) It's a bit of a walk there, I shan't say it isn't. But it's nice and bright, clean too. She'll be friendly enough when she gets to know us, I'm sure of that.

Hetty (*unmoved*) They don't like us in their places. They want young 'uns what look lively. Come in, have a big dinner and leave in ten minutes, that's what they want. (*She pauses*) I got a letter this morning.

Dolly From Daisy was it? Amy's late again. Meeting that Harold Kingham I shouldn't wonder. Do you know, I saw the two of them yesterday afternoon, walking along holding hands. Holding hands, Het! Can you imagine!

Hetty It wasn't from Daisy. It was from the Housing.

Dolly I don't think it's dignified, Het, not at her age. (*She pauses*) The Housing did you say?

Hetty They're offering me a flat in Leyton.

Dolly (*after a pause, decisively*) It'll be one of them nobody else wants.

Hetty Why?

Dolly Well, you don't think they'd give a perfectly good flat to a pensioner do you?

Hetty But it's close to Daisy. They're taking me to see it this afternoon.

Dolly Hmmm. They have a lot of trouble in Leyton — with the kids. Much worse than in Hackney they say.

Hetty Oh dear!

Dolly And all them narrow dark streets and viaducts. (*She sucks in her breath*) I shouldn't think it's very safe round there on your own.

Hetty But it's ground floor, with a little garden.

Dolly Well, I won't try to put you off, Het, but it only makes it easy for them, being on the ground floor.

Hetty looks baffled

Burglars, Het, burglars.

Hetty (*frightened*) Oo! But the garden, Dolly; I could have a pet.

Dolly Do you know, I was reading in the Gazette about a woman who was mugged in Leyton. A pensioner she was, like us. They left her with a broken arm and a black eye, and made off with her bag. All she had in it was her pension book and three pound. Shocking, ennit?

Hetty We're none of us safe are we? You'd think after all we've been through, they'd at least leave us alone when we get old.

Dolly I know, Het. You put up with it all when you're younger 'cause you think you can take it easy when you get to our age. But it isn't like that is it? When you've had it hard all your life it don't just stop one day do it? If it's not one thing it's another.

Hetty It's no life for us old 'uns. No-one wants to know and they don't care neither. A nuisance, that's all we are.

Dolly True enough. We've only got each other now.

Hetty You're right, Dolly. I've only got Daisy for all the comfort she is and not a soul else. She never married you see, didn't Daisy, and we didn't have no kids, on account of his war wounds, poor George.

Dolly We didn't want any till it was too late.

Hetty We've got no-one.

Dolly Not a living soul since my Bill passed on, God rest his soul. (*She pauses*) Anyway, you listen to your friends, Het, and have a good think before you go traipsing off. I mean, we've been in Hackney all our lives haven't we? And don't you let them bully you into settling where it suits 'em, them Housing people.

Hetty I'm not so sure now, Dolly. But I need to move from where I'm living. Do you think they'd move me somewhere else, but still in Hackney?

Dolly Do you know, I'm sure they would, Het.

Hetty I'll tell 'em then, this afternoon shall I?

Dolly That's right, Het.

Hetty I think I should eat something now. I didn't have no dinner last night you see. Oh, I did feel bad. (*To the counter*) Can I have a fried sausage and a slice, lady?

Dolly And two cups of tea please.

Amy enters, flustered

Amy Hello, ducks! Here I am. (*To the counter*) Tea please, dearie.

Hetty What's up, dear?

Amy Why? Flushed am I? Got reason to be.

Dolly (*disapprovingly*) Been with that Harold Kingham?

Amy As it happens, yes I have.

Dolly (*disapprovingly*) See you walking down the street yesterday, holding hands.

Amy (*unabashed*) That's right.

The Waitress brings Hetty's food and the cups of tea. Hetty begins to eat

Dolly (*sighing*) It's beyond me what you see in Harold Kingham, he's not right in the head for a start. (*She thinks awhile*) Do you know, from the day my Bill passed on I never looked at another man. I felt it'd be an insult to his memory. And I'd feel I was being unfaithful, no matter how long he'd been gone. 'Cause he was a good 'un my Bill. Funny isn't it? (*She pauses*) Do you know, even now I still feel he's with me, looking over me shoulder and saying

"Go on, Dolly, you're all right. I'm here", just like he used to.

Amy (*momentarily moved*) I know what you mean, but if my Fred could talk to me now, he'd say "you enjoy yourself girl, never mind about me". He was good like that was my Fred, never minded me staying on the stage after we was married. I know he'd want me to do whatever'd make me happy now. That's why I said yes to Harry.

Hetty Yes to what dear?

Dolly Yeah, yes to what?

Amy He proposed, I said yes.

Dolly (*incredulously*) What! Marriage?

Amy Of course marriage.

Dolly What do you want to go and get married for?

Hetty They say he's got a nice flat in Bethnal Green, with a garden. And he's got a little dog.

Amy That's right—Dora.

Dolly DOR . . . He's mad! May the Good Lord forgive him!

Hetty They'll most like have your picture in the Gazette, getting married at your a . . .

Amy Yes, I suppose they will. I was well known round here once.

Dolly Well, you're as crazy as he is, that's all I've got to say. (*She pauses*) Moving into his place are you?

Amy 'Course. So anyway, this'll be by way of a cheerio.

Dolly Why, what's your hurry?

Amy Well, we'll be married soon enough. No sense in playing the innocent is there?

Dolly Amy Johnson!

Hetty What do you mean, dear?

Dolly It's downright sinful, that's what it is.

Amy Oh, don't talk such rubbish.

Dolly No, it is. No matter nothing'll happen; it's still a sin.

Amy How do you know nothing'll happen?

Dolly Oh, you're disgusting!

Amy Anyway we'll have the flat all lovely-looking in time for the wedding.

Hetty What's sinful, dear?

Dolly Oh, never mind!

The Lights fade to a Black-out

SCENE 3

The same. Thursday

Hetty and Dolly are again seated at their table drinking tea

Hetty She won't be coming then.

Dolly She'll be in Bethnal Green now, living in sin.

Hetty Oh dear!

Dolly What does a woman of her age want to gad about for, all
    dressed up and caked in make-up. Well, if you can't show your
    God-given face at seventy-two I say it's very sad.

Hetty Didn't she say she was sixty-five, dear?

Dolly (*ignoring Hetty*) Chasing after a man like a girl of twenty!
    Do you know, I just couldn't do with a man under my feet now. I
    reckon it'd finish me off!

Hetty You get used to being on your own don't you?

Dolly You do, Het. Just me and me cat. I couldn't be bothered with
    a man.

Hetty It's nice to have a pet.

Dolly Do you know, it'd make me feel sick if a man wanted to
    touch me now.

Hetty What man, dear?

Dolly Never mind. (*She pauses, sipping tea*) She never invited us to
    the wedding, did you notice that?

Hetty 'Cause she's younger do you think? They don't want us.

Dolly She's seventy-two, Het! How many more times! Still, you're
    right in a way. She's having her second childhood that one. Do
    you know, she's living in a fool's world. Like that film, what was
    it? *Sunset Boulevard* with Gloria Swanson. She went mad in the
    end.

Hetty Oh dear. (*She pauses, confused*) But I saw her on the telly
    only last week, Dolly.

Dolly Oh, shut up, Het! (*There is a longer pause*) I went down again
    yesterday. To have another look and get to know the lady. Jane
    they call her but I don't reckon that's her real name, it don't
    sound I-talian to me.

Hetty Who, dear?

Dolly The woman in the caff, in Mare Street. Do you know, once you get used to the route it's not a long walk at all. I like it there, Het. (*Whispering*) They're more friendly than here. Take a real interest they do.

Hetty (*unhappily*) Oh.

Dolly We'll meet in there then shall we? It'll be better without Amy really, and all her talk of the theatre.

Hetty (*bravely*) I saw it, the flat. It's — very nice. All modern with a pink bathroom and handles on the side of the bath and a mat so's you don't slip. Lovely garden it's got too. They say I can have a pet, no trouble. Only round the corner from Daisy.

Dolly Hmmm. Bit funny all the same, find you a flat so quick. Did you tell them you wanted to stay in Hackney?

Hetty No, dear.

Dolly I don't suppose you'll write to 'em neither.

Hetty I took it, dear.

There is a pause

Dolly I thought you might.

Hetty I'm going to the pet shop later to get a cat. Come with me if you like. (*She pauses*) I thought, now that Amy's gone, it wouldn't have been the same anyhow, dear, would it?

Dolly Nothing stays the same, Het, that's the trouble.

Hetty Besides you've got your clubs. Anyway, I'll write to you and you can write back.

Dolly I can't write, Het, me hands shake too much.

Hetty Don't suppose you could get over to Leyton-way some-times, dear?

Dolly Don't suppose I could.

Hetty Only I can't manage a distance with me legs.

Dolly I know.

There is a pause

Hetty I'm sorry if I'm leaving you on your own, Dolly. Only you know they don't care about us old 'uns; we've got to look out for ourselves.

Dolly I know, Het. We'd have left each other anyway, one way or another.

Hetty What do you mean, Dolly?

Dolly Only that you can't hold on to things forever. You think you've got 'em for good and nothing can change but it does.

Your life comes in on the crest of a wave and you have to hurry to enjoy it before the tide goes out. Then all that's left is a few flimsy scraps of nothing.

Hetty What are you saying, dear? I don't understand. Are you all right?

Dolly All you have left are memories. Not much to leave behind of a whole life is it? And memories change or fade. You make them what you want them to be, till they're nothing to do with real things at all. You pull up your roots and there's nothing there but dust.

Hetty Dolly, why are you talking like this?

Dolly Never mind, Het. I'm just thinking of all that's been and gone. All the people we've known who've died.

Hetty Oh, dear me, yes!

Dolly All the people you've got your roots in; your parents, your husband. They all go in the end and leave you behind, as if it should teach you something.

Hetty Tut, tut.

Dolly Do you know, when you're dead they don't bury you in them big satin-lined coffins. They take you out and crate you up, stuffed in with newspaper, did you know that? They probably use that same coffin for years, like a display package in Woolworths.

Hetty (*not having listened to Dolly's last speech*) I've seen 'em go all right. One by one. My George, Amy's Fred, Dora Kingham, Stan Roberts, your Bill . . . Dolly, what will you do now?

Dolly I'll manage, Het. (*She pats Hetty's hand*) I'll manage. (*Her hand rests on Hetty's during a pause, then she turns to the counter*) Two more cups of tea—please.

They both look away, in opposite directions, towards the Audience

The Lights fade to a Black-out

SCENE 4

The same. Saturday, the following week

Dolly is sitting alone, reading the back page of the Gazette and finishing her tea. After a moment, when she has read the page, she puts the paper down. She glances around then looks to the door, half expecting someone she knows to come in. No-one does. She picks up the paper again but has read it all. There is a pause

Dolly (*to the counter*) Last day today, isn't it, dear?

There is no reply throughout her speech

Shame. I'll miss this place. Do you know, I been coming here sixteen year? Been a caff for — oh — a long time, this has. Course you've only been here, what, five year? (*Pause*) Well I'll be off soon. Paid for me tea didn't I? (*Pause*) You'll be glad to see the back of me won't you? Just like everyone else. I suppose you think we don't keep ourselves clean or something. Well, do you know, I polish my shoes every day before I come out? How often do you hear of that nowadays? (*Pause*) Ah, youngsters. You just want to ignore us. Disgusted to think you'll be like me one day I shouldn't wonder. (*She sniffs*) No, you're not the sort. Think of old age like other people think of accidents — it'll never happen to you! I know. (*Pause*) Ah well, I'll have to go. I've got plenty to see to, you know — I don't have no home helps. Yes. There's always housework and washing and looking after Fluffy. There's always a lot to do. (*She pauses a while*) Yes. There's always a lot to do. (*After a longer pause she slowly gets to her feet and begins to trundle out*)

Amy enters when Dolly is half-way to the door

They look at each other in obvious delight and make a movement as if to hug, but quickly check it

Dolly Amy!
Amy Hoped I'd catch you. To say a proper good-bye.
Dolly I was just going.
Amy Got time for a tea, ducks? Last cuppa together?
Dolly Course I have.

They both settle in seats

Thought you'd be in Bethnal Green by now.
Amy (*smiling wearily; to the counter*) Two cups of tea, lovey, please. (*She surveys the café*) Last day isn't it?
Dolly Yes. I was just saying — well, thinking really — it's been a caff here for as long as I can remember.

Amy Old Pat and Stan used to run it.

Amy Oh yes. Pat and Stan. (*She casts her mind back and smiles*) He was a card he was. The stories he used to tell!

Amy I remember — talk about sauce!

Dolly But do you know, they said he made them up.

Amy 'Course he did, but they weren't half funny all the same. Do you remember his laugh?

Dolly Oo yes, and his big tummy shaking with it, up and down, side to side, just like a blooming jelly.

They laugh as the teas are brought by the Waitress

Amy (*soberly*) Poor Stan. I'll always remember his face, so jolly, them fat rosy cheeks.

Dolly He was the picture of health, God rest his soul. Who'd have thought he could go so quick?

Amy He always made you feel welcome, didn't he? And poor Pat. She was lost without him. (*She thinks of herself; then*) No-one heard from her after she sold up and moved away.

Dolly Hmm. She tried but she couldn't cope on her own. I never knew of a bloke like her Stan. Such a big man who could work so quick. If he wasn't doing this, he was doing that, laughing and telling jokes all the while. Always had a friendly word for everyone.

Amy You don't find many like him, that's for sure. (*She pauses*) Het been and gone has she?

Dolly (*uneasily*) No. She's moving away, Amy.

Amy What?

Dolly The Housing got her a place near her Daisy's.

Amy They never did! After all this time?

Dolly Hmm. Thought she might come in to say goodbye. Haven't seen her since last week. (*Bracing herself*) Still, I expect she's busy packing.

Amy Yes, but I'm sure she'll come in today, Dolly, to say goodbye.

Dolly I'm not so sure. You know what a scatterbrain she is. Poor Hetty. She's always been a good friend to me. I'll miss her. (*Looking up*) I'll miss you, too, Amy.

Amy (*looking down at the table*) Will you?

Dolly 'Course. Mind you, I was getting bored with your talk of the theatre. Be glad not to listen to that no more I says. But I was wrong. It brought back a bit of life, a bit of the old times.

Amy The old times are dead and gone, Dol.
Dolly Maybe so, but ... When is it you're going then?
Amy What?
Dolly Bethnal Green way. Won't see you then, I expect.

There is a pause. Dolly eyes Amy who is downcast

Come on girl, I didn't mean to make you feel bad. All that about
missing you. (*She tries another tack*) I don't want you going off
feeling sorry for me, Amy Johnson — you know I won't have any
of that!
Amy (*wearily*) It's not that, Dolly. I'm not going to Bethnal Green.
Dolly (*understandingly*) Oh. It's off then — between you and ... and
him?
Amy Yes, it's off.
Dolly (*gently reproachful*) Well, it's about time you saw some sense.
Amy Sense? Sense didn't have much to do with it. (*Pause*) It was so
much like being with my Fred again you see. And he said he was
lonely; going to be all alone at Christmas. I felt sorry for him.
Dolly Well, do you know, men just can't take to being on their
own. Go all to pieces they do. I think that's why God generally
takes 'em first, dear.
Amy Well, I get lonely too, Dolly, and it ain't no easier for me than
for them.
Dolly (*patting Amy's hand*) I know, Amy. I know.
Amy I take my picture album out sometimes. I look at the pictures
of me and my Fred, think of all the times we had. It's so real I
nearly can't believe that part of my life's finished — gone for
good. That I won't see my Fred no more. Then I have a good long
cry.
Dolly Do you, Amy? I always do the same yet in all these years
we never said.
Amy You still miss your Bill then, Dolly?
Dolly More every day. I take his picture off the sideboard and hold
it. I cry meself to sleep holding it sometimes. Next day I feel worse
and better. Worse because I miss him more and better because all
that love's got to get through to him somehow. 'Cause he's still
with me, around, somewhere — always will be.
Amy It's cruel, ennit? (*Pause*) It's because I couldn't bear it I ...
Dolly I know.
Amy I went to his house — to look it over. We sat down on the

settee for a cuddle. (*She looks at Dolly*) I don't care. I wanted to close my eyes and pretend he was my Fred. Before I could though, he says "I want love". "Not yet", I says, 'cause that ain't what I wanted. "Come on", he said, "give us a kiss and you'll feel inclined". I only want holding I told him. (*Acutely embarrassed*) "Well then, bugger off!", he said. Then I left.

Dolly (*shaking her head*) Oh, Amy love.

Amy I know. Now. It was just that . . . I just wanted . . .

Dolly (*patting Amy's hand again*) Never mind, Amy dear, we've got our memories.

Amy Have we? Is that all?

Dolly It's not much I know, but it's all we've got. Anyhow, Amy, the show must go on.

Amy Must it?

Dolly (*firmly*) Yes, Amy. Yes, it must.

They look at each other in understanding

   Hetty enters

Hetty Hello, dears.

Amy Het! Not gone yet?

Hetty Dolly told you then, dear. (*She trundles to her seat*)

Dolly Come to say goodbye have you? Well come on then — I want to tell you something.

Hetty All right, dear, I'm nearly there. (*She sits heavily*) Oof!

Dolly About Amy. She . . . (*Looking at Amy*) She changed her mind. About Harold.

Hetty (*confused*) Did you, dear? Oh. (*To the counter*) Tea please, lady.

Amy (*quickly*) How's your legs today, Het?

Hetty Me legs? They're all right.

Dolly and Amy look at Hetty in astonishment

   (*Thinking*) I don't blame you, dear. They're all right but they take a lot of looking after.

Dolly Who do, men?

Hetty No. Dogs, dear. I'm not so keen meself. I prefer a cat. Be going down the pet shop this afternoon.

Dolly Didn't you go last week then?

Hetty I only looked in the window. (*Concentrating*) Only how will I get her home? Will she be all right in me shopping bag do you think?

Dolly Well, I don't know.

Amy They'll give you a box, but you'll have to pay for it. About a pound I think, and it's only cardboard.

Hetty Oh dear!

Dolly Tut, tut. Do you know, Hetty dear, the kitten will cost you seven or eight pound?

Hetty Seven or eight pound?

Dolly I'm afraid so.

The Waitress beings Hetty's tea

Hetty I think I can manage that.

Amy Are you sure?

Hetty Yes. It's not too much to pay for a little life and companion is it, dear?

Dolly That's true. My Fluffy's worth her weight in gold.

Hetty Course she is. (*Pause*) Did you see that cat show on the telly last night? Ooh, I did enjoy it, and I says to meself . . . (*Remembering last week's conversation*) Ooh, Amy, that was real wasn't it? I mean, what you said . . .

Amy (*realizing*) Oh that! Don't worry, Het, *that* was real, all right.

Hetty Thought it was. You was pulling me leg then — about Elsie? Having a joke wasn't you, dear?

Dolly and Amy exchange tolerant glances

Amy Yes, lovey, I was having you on.

Hetty (*chuckling good-humouredly*) You shouldn't play jokes on me, dear. I don't always catch on, you know.

Dolly (*smiling*) We know, Het.

There is a relaxed pause

Amy Well? Let's have your news then.

Hetty What news, dear?

Amy About Leyton. All packed and ready?

Hetty No. I been at Daisy's. Them Social people took me.

Amy Well, you want to make a start soon.

Hetty (*absent-mindedly*) Hmm.

Dolly How's Daisy?

Hetty She got a shock. Went all into a panic, dear, because I upset her routine.

Dolly Ooh, don't tell me your Daisy wasn't glad to see you.

Hetty 'Course she was. We haven't seen each other for near on a year. Only she has times for everything you see. This at eleven o'clock, that at twelve, sleeping at two till four. (*She pauses*) I got there quarter past three.

Amy Well it must have been nice for you all the same.

Hetty (*untruthfully*) Oh yes. (*Thinking*) She's still bossy. Still the little madam. She was forever telling me what to do when we were girls. She ain't changed much now.

Dolly Do you know, Het, it don't sound like you got on too well.

Hetty (*knitting her brows*) She's always busy, Daisy is. Writes a lot of letters to the papers. (*She pauses*) I was quite glad to get home really.

Amy (*smiling*) Do you need any help with your packing?

Hetty No, dear.

Amy I suppose the Social Services will sort out your big pieces? They'll shift the lot over for you.

Hetty Hmm. I started taking out my things and putting them on me big table. Things I forgot I had, dear. (*Pause*) I polished all me ornaments off me mantleshelf, and I took me pictures off the wall. Then I looks up to where me wedding picture used to hang. The paper there was a different colour. It give me quite a turn. All new looking it was. Took me back to when we was decorating, me and George . . . (*Pause*)

Dolly What's up, Het?

Hetty It wasn't right, dear. I put everything straight back in its place. I can't explain but I belong in me little flat, after all these years, that's all. I can't go to no new house in no Leyton.

Amy What about Daisy?

Hetty Truth be told, we never got on, me and Daisy.

Dolly And the kids?

Hetty Ah, they ain't so bad if I don't holler at 'em dear.

Amy And the stairs?

Hetty Well, you can't have everything, can you?

Amy (*affectionately*) Oh, Het!

Hetty And then I sees that cat show on the telly and I says to meself—sod 'em. Sod 'em I says! I'll get my cat, dears, and I'll get her one of them trays. I'll put down some newspaper and let her out on the balcony. And she can sit at the windowsill if she likes. She'll get enough air won't she, dear?

Dolly (*laughing; putting her hand over Hetty's*) Dear Hetty!

Hetty (*patting Dolly's hand in return*) And poor old Dolly. Thought we'd all go off and leave you, didn't you?

Dolly sniffs, and quickly pulls out her hanky to dab her eyes

Amy Now, now ducks—none of that. There ain't no cause.

Dolly (*recovering*) Do you know, I went down last week, to see about one of them homes.

Amy Dolly!

Dolly I never expected you'd come back you see. I still can hardly believe it.

Amy Well, we're here now.

Dolly But how long for?

Amy (*reproachfully*) Dolly.

Dolly Yes, I know, but it's knocks all the way in life isn't it, till you come to expect them. So when a helping hand comes along . . .

Amy Don't give us that now! You've never needed a helping hand in your life!

Dolly I've managed—but it isn't the same thing. Is it?

Hetty What home, dear?

Dolly Old people's home, Het.

Hetty (*distastefully*) Ooh, don't go to one of them places, dear.

Dolly They wouldn't take me anyway—not whilst I can take care of meself.

Hetty They're like prisons them places. No, worse. Like horspidals. Once you go in you don't never come out again.

Amy Just as well, you know, because you couldn't have taken Fluffy.

Dolly Couldn't . . .?

Amy No. They'd tell you to have her put down. They don't allow pets in those homes.

Dolly (*surprised*) Put down? (*With anger; defiantly*) Put down my Fluffy! I never would!

Hetty Put her down where, dear?

Amy (*irritated*) Oh, Het! Shut up!

There is a pause

Hetty Here, I nearly forgot to have me breakfast. (*To the counter*)

Fried sausage and a slice please, lady.

Amy And three more cups of tea.

They turn back to Dolly

Dolly (*timidly*) Right, well ... (*Gathering her strength; smiling*) What about this caff in Mare Street then?

They all smile

The Lights fade

CURTAIN

FURNITURE AND PROPERTY LIST

SCENE 1

On stage: Table. *On it:* cup of tea
Three chairs
Counter. *Behind it:* cup of tea for Hetty, plate with sausage and
bread for Hetty, cup of tea for Amy, plate with fried egg and
bread for Hetty
Other dressing at Producer's discretion

Personal: **Dolly:** newspaper, handbag
Hetty: handbag
Amy: handbag

SCENE 2

Strike: Dirty crockery from table

Set: Two cups of tea on table
Plate of sausage and bread behind counter

SCENE 3

Strike: Dirty crockery

Set: Two cups of tea on table

SCENE 4

Strike: Dirty cups

Set: Cup of tea on table
Three cups of tea behind counter

Personal: **Dolly:** newspaper, handkerchief

LIGHTING PLOT

A café interior. No practical fittings required

SCENE 1
To open: general lighting

Cue 1   **Dolly:** ". . . that caff in Mare Street."   (Page 6)
        Slow fade to Black-out

SCENE 2
To open: general lighting

Cue 2   **Dolly:** "Oh, never mind!"   (Page 9)
        Slow fade to Black-out

SCENE 3
To open: general lighting

Cue 3   **Dolly:** "Two more cups of tea, please."   (Page 12)
        Slow fade to Black-out

SCENE 4
To open: general lighting

Cue 4   They all smile.   (Page 20)
        Fade to Black-out

MADE AND PRINTED IN GREAT BRITAIN BY
LATIMER TREND & COMPANY LTD PLYMOUTH

MADE IN ENGLAND